JUMPSTART!
NUMERACY

MATHS ACTIVITIES AND GAMES FOR AGES 5–14

John Taylor

 David Fulton Publishers

This edition reprinted 2006 by Routledge
2 Park Square, Milton Park, Abingdon, Oxon, OX14 4RN
Simultaneously published in the USA and Canada
By Routledge
270 Madison Avenue, New York, NY 10016

First published in Great Britain in 2004 by David Fulton Publishers
Reprinted 2006 (twice)

10 9 8 7 6 5 4

British Library Cataloguing in Publication Data
A catalogue record for this book is available from the British Library.

ISBN 1 84312 264 2

Typeset by Mark Heslington, Scarborough, North Yorkshire
Cover Design by Martin Cater
Printed and bound in Great Britain

Contents

Acknowledgements

Many people have helped to bring me in various ways to writing this book.

There are all the colleagues and children I've worked with over the years who have coped with my idiosyncrasies, inspired my creativity and strengthened my belief that fun is a crucial part of learning.

My supportive family over the years has provided encouragement, and at home a place of sanity in an increasingly mad world. Quietly tolerating my writing schedule and punctuating it with copious quantities of tea has been a great help. Before my daughters were able to safely brew tea they unwittingly contributed in other ways. I still remember as if it were yesterday reassuring a colleague that a new resource I'd made had been '. . . tried out on the tame eight-year-old I keep at home'. Who would have thought that many years on my older daughter Alison would proofread this book for me!

There is a growing community of Internet-friendly teachers around the world who freely exchange resources, ideas, problems and solutions through Internet newsgroups. A recent query was responded to within hours by people as far afield as Germany and Canada. In particular, thanks are due to David Dixon of Ontario.

Encouragement also comes from some of the users of my teachers' resource website, www.johnandgwyn.co.uk, who take the time to email comments and suggestions.

Finally I am grateful to Ginn, part of Harcourt Education, who had the courage and trust to take on an unpublished unknown to write *Maths Express* back in 1999.

Introduction

The activities in this book are mainly intended as warm-up activities during the first part of a maths lesson. The intention is to encourage participation in an atmosphere of fun, mutual support and tolerance.

In Key Stages 1 and 2, where time is more flexible, they can help you to make constructive use of the otherwise 'slack' few minutes between planned activities.

The activities vary in style. Some are verbal games played around a circle, during which players are gradually eliminated down to the last few survivors. Others are played as teams, sometimes collaborating, sometimes in turn. If you don't like the format of the game used for one activity you can use another game format instead. For example: if you don't want to use a team format for ordering numbers (as in **Order Them**), you could use the individual-based format of **Number Snap**.

Some of the activities require no resource other than yourself, while some need simple flashcard type resources to be prepared. Other activities make use of a computer and interactive whiteboard, running an easy-to-type Excel spreadsheet file. Some people shy away from using Excel, thinking that its usefulness is restricted to producing balance sheets and budgets. However, it is a fantastically versatile tool for educational use that is overlooked by far too many techno-phobic teachers. For examples of resources using Excel, visit my website, *John Taylor's Freebies* at www.johnandgwyn.co.uk.

An ICT Tips and Hints section is included in this book, partly to avoid repetition of instructions; but also to extend the use of computers as an everyday classroom tool. The cardinal rule of using the computer files material is to prepare and save it beforehand.

In order to use the random number generator feature in Excel, as suggested in a number of the activities, you will need to enable the **Analysis ToolPak Add-In**. This is simple to do, and there are instructions to help you in ICT Tips and Hints **(Chapter 6)**.

Table of Games

Chapter 1 Number

Name	Activity	👤	☠	👤	👤	🎵	💻
Number Snap	recognition of numerals and numbers	1					
Number Lotto	recognition of numerals and numbers	1					✓
How Many?	estimating numbers of objects	1	2				
The Matchstick Game	patterns, odds and evens, addition and subtraction, and much more		2	3	4	5	
Order Them	ordering numbers mentally	1	2	3	4		
Beanbag Count	counting on in 1s, 2s, 3s, 4s, 5s and 10s	1	2				
Animal Count	adding and subtracting 1, 2 and 4 mentally	1	2				
Town/Country/Team Count	add and subtract 1, 2, 3, 4, 5 mentally		2	3	4		
Number Bond Countdown	recall of number bonds	1	2				
Odds and Evens	identifying odd and even numbers	1	2				
Stand Up and Be Counted (1)	place value with integers		2	3	4	5	✓
Stand Up and Be Counted (2)	place value with integers and decimals			3	4	5	✓
Make a Number	making numbers out of numerals		2	3	4		✓

Name	Activity						
First Team Home	quick mental computation of addition and subtraction equations		2	3			
League Table (1)	quick mental creation and computation of number equations			3	4		
League Table (2)	quick mental creation and computation of number equations including negative numbers				4	5	
Join Up (2)	addition of sets	1	2	3			
Target Totals (1)	addition		2	3	4		
Target Totals (2)	addition		2	3	4		
Halves and Doubles	halving and doubling						
Number Cricket (1)	doubling numbers, totals to 5 digits				4	5	
Number Cricket (2)	halving numbers, up to 4 digits				4	5	
Number Rounders	sequential doubling		2	3	4		
Double Up	doubling up, totals up to 4 digits			3	4	5	
Eights and Nines	using shortcuts to quickly add and subtract 9 and 8 mentally			3	4	5	
Eighties and Nineties	using shortcuts to quickly add and subtract 90 and 80 mentally			3	4	5	

Chapter 4 Shape and Space

Name	Activity	😊	👧👧	😊	😊	😊	🖥
Shape Lotto	recognition of regular shapes	1	2				
Shape Snap	recognition of regular shapes	1	2	3			
Triangle Lotto	classification of different types of triangle			3	4		
Treasure Hunt (1)	letter and number coordinates		2	3			
Treasure Hunt (2)	2-digit number coordinates		2	3			
Treasure Hunt (3)	2-digit number coordinates, all four quadrants				4	5	
Pipeline (1)	directions		2	3	4		
Don't Lose Your Bearings	bearings				4	5	
Pipeline (2)	coordinates		2	3	4		
Pipeline (3)	coordinates in all four quadrants				4		
Chicken Pen	perimeter and area		2	3	4		
Shape up	perimeter and area of polygons			3	4		

Chapter 5 Data Handling

Name	Activity	 R & Y1	Y2 & Y3	Y4 & Y5	Y6 & Y7	Y8 & Y9	ICT
Name A ... (1)	Venn diagrams	1	2				
Name A ... (2)	Carroll diagrams	1	2				
Shape Sort	Carroll diagrams		2	3			
Data Relay	quick processing of mean, median, mode and range			3	4	5	
Probability Brainstorm	probability				4	5	

KEY:

R & Y1   Y2 &Y3

Y4 & Y5   Y6 & Y7

Y8 &Y9   includes ICT suggestions/ instructions

CHAPTER 1

Number

NUMBER SNAP

RECOGNITION OF NUMERALS AND NUMBERS

This is a refinement of the game 'Snap'. The children start off standing up on the carpet. The first child to identify each correct match, by raising a hand and calling out 'Snap!' sits down. Play continues until all the children are seated.

You will require a set of cards with the numbers you wish to practise, with plenty of multiples; or else use a PC or laptop computer, with or without interactive whiteboard to generate snap cards on screen – it's very easy!

 To make your own computer Snap game follow these simple instructions:

- Open up MS Excel.
- Type in 1 in cell A1, and a *higher number* (e.g. 15) in B1.
- In cells D8 and F8 type in
  =RANDBETWEEN(A1,B1)
- Increase the font size for cells D8 and F8, widen columns D and F and make row 8 taller – **Chapter 6** will tell you how if you don't know.
- Put a border around cells D8 and F8 and perhaps change the background and foreground colours to make them stand out.

Each time you press the (F9) key two random numbers will appear. These will be between the numbers written in cells A1 and B1. If a **#** appears in place of a number just widen the column.

Variations
- Raise the minimum number generated by making the number in cell A1 higher than 1. *Note*: The value in B1 must be greater than the value in A1.
- Raise the maximum number by increasing the value in cell B1.

Note: as you increase the values typed into cells A1 and B1 you reduce the frequency of the numbers displayed coinciding.

NUMBER LOTTO

RECOGNITION OF NUMERALS AND NUMBERS

You need 40 or more numbered cards, with duplicates, e.g. at least 4 × cards 1–10 or 2 × cards 1–20. Place them face down on the carpet in rows.

Each child has a go at turning over two matching cards. If they match, the child keeps them and becomes a spectator. If they don't match the cards are turned face down again.

When all the cards have been paired up, ask, 'Who found a pair with their first go?' 'Who took two turns?' 'Three turns?' etc.

Variations
- Increase the number of cards available by adding more pairs.

- Have two games going on at once, racing to see which group of players finishes first (without cheating!).

This game is also good for spatial awareness and short-term memory.

HOW MANY?

ESTIMATING NUMBERS OF OBJECTS

Label tables or areas of the floor to indicate number ranges such as

'fewer than 5', 'between 5 and 10', 'between 10 and 20' and 'more than 20'

Have ready prepared but hidden from view, illustrations showing different numbers of shapes or drawings of objects. Show an illustration to the children for a few seconds then hide it again. The children then go and sit in the area in whose range they think the illustration falls.

The children in the correct group are given a Unifix® or similar cube each to keep as an indication of their score. The children collect these for each correct answer and stick them together. Play continues through a series of illustrations. At the end the children hold up their Unifix® sticks and compare the lengths to show who has earned the most.

Variations
- Use collections of objects such as a handful of cubes, bundle of pencils, small tub of marbles, string of linked paper clips, etc.

3

- Vary the amount of time allowed to look, counting out in seconds, which will disrupt them from trying to count.
- Use illustrations that vary in size.
- Hold up (for example) an illustration with squares and triangles, and ask, 'How many triangles?'.

THE MATCHSTICK GAME

PATTERNS, ODDS AND EVENS, ADDITION AND SUBTRACTION, AND MUCH MORE!

In more years than I care to mention working in education, this is the game I have used, and still use, the most. I was taught it by one of the locals, one rainy lunchtime in 1973, at the Stag Inn in the village of Dufton, Cumbria. It was probably the most useful thing I learnt during teacher training! My student colleague and I made two pints last an hour as we watched the landlord wallpapering the tiny lounge bar between serving customers.

You begin with fifteen 'matches' (or cubes, counters, etc.), or you can draw them on a whiteboard. You lay them out as shown. There are just two rules:

1. When it's your turn you can remove as many matchsticks as you like, so long as they are in the same row.
2. To win you must leave the other player (or team) with the last match.

There are to my knowledge five patterns that you can leave your opponent with which will virtually guarantee you winning, and so players begin to anticipate and plan ahead. The commonest are leaving: 2 rows of 2, 2 rows of 3, an odd number of single matchsticks, and a sequence of 1, 2 and 3.

Initially in the teaching situation the game is best played as two teams, using a whiteboard (or good old-fashioned blackboard). At its simplest level you let team members take turns at making their team's move. Much discussion on team tactics takes place while the player holding the board-wiper ponders which matchstick(s) to rub out.

Once the pupils are hooked on the game you can introduce alternative ways of deciding who takes the team's turn, such as asking the team a tables question, an addition equation, the square of a particular number, etc. Because the game is so quick there is time for several rounds and few can remember (or care) which team won more games.

The game can also be played by individuals, and doesn't require specialised equipment; though I would avoid using live matches unless you are playing in the Stag Inn, Dufton!

Variations
- Play the basic game without questions with four teams in a knockout competition – two semi-finals, a final, and a runners-up final.
- Vary the type of questions required to earn the right to take your team's move.
- Exclude those who have had a turn from answering another question until all the team have had a go.

ORDER THEM

ORDERING NUMBERS MENTALLY

This can be played either with a set of flashcards, as used in **Number Lotto**, or by using a computer as described below.

Divide the group into teams.

If using cards: shuffle them up and deal five, placing them on a ledge to display them.

If using a computer, simply press the (F9) key.

As soon as the children can see all five numbers they order them mentally and shoot up their hands to offer an answer on behalf of their team. When asked they must give the numbers in value order – any delay in answering passes on to someone from another group.

Two points for a successful first attempt, one point if it's been passed over to another team.

First team to score a predetermined number of points wins.

Note: In some instances duplicates of the numbers appear, this is not a problem, they simply give the answer for example as '3, 6, 6, 9, 10'.

 To make your own computer ordering game follow these simple instructions:

- Open up MS Excel.
- In three, four, or five non-adjoining cells type in **=RANDBETWEEN(0,9)**. Using cells that are not in

the same row or column will make it slightly more difficult.
- Adjust the font size and column widths if necessary, as described in **Chapter 6**.

Variations
- Order the numbers in descending order.
- Select six or seven numbers at a time.
- Use higher numbers by putting a higher value in cell A1.

Display the flashcards by sticking them on a display surface in random positions using Blu-Tack® or a similar product.

BEANBAG COUNT

COUNTING ON IN 1s, 2s, 3s, 4s, 5s AND 10s

Everyone (grown-ups included!) sits on the carpet in a circle. Play is started by the first player, who calls out 'zero' and throws the beanbag underarm to someone who is seated roughly opposite. The player who catches it must call out the next number in the chosen sequence and throw the beanbag across the circle to the player sitting to the left of the person who threw it to them. Thus the throws go back and forth across the circle, rotating around clockwise.

In its simplest form the objective is to reach a target number without dropping the beanbag, or to see how high a number is reached before it is dropped.

Variations
- Count on in 2s, 3s, 4s, 5s and 10s.
- Play the game counting backwards, or simply reverse when a target number is reached.

- Eliminate players (including grown-ups!) who drop the beanbag.
- Throw the beanbag randomly so that players can't predict when it's going to be their turn to catch and re-throw it.

ANIMAL COUNT

ADDING AND SUBTRACTING 1,2 AND 4 MENTALLY

The children (and adults!) sit in a circle. The first player starts off by saying a number followed by the name of an animal (e.g. '5, elephant'). The next player (clockwise in the circle) adds on the number of syllables in the name of the previous animal, and gives the new total and a new animal name. For example 'dog' = add 1, 'tiger' = add 2, elephant = add 3, caterpillar = add 4, hippopotamus = add 5.

A typical sequence of turns might be:

> '5, elephant', '8, tiger', '10, goldfish', '12, caterpillar', '16, hedgehog'

Players who give an incorrect answer or are 'timed out' are eliminated until the end of the current game.

Play on until an agreed number of players are left, or until a countdown timer has gone off.

Variations
- Restrict animal names to an agreed set, displayed in words and/or pictures.
- Reverse the direction of play on your command to keep everyone alert.
- Subtract the number of syllables from the total when playing anti-clockwise.

TOWN / COUNTRY / TEAM COUNT

ADD AND SUBTRACT 1, 2, 3, 4, 5 MENTALLY

This is played as Animal Count but with the following modifications:

- Names of towns, cities or football teams are used instead of animals.
- Using a town/country/team that has already been used puts the 'guilty' player out of the current game.
- Strict observance of an agreed time limit for responses.

Variations
- Restrict towns to a geographical area (e.g. UK, Europe).
- Reverse the direction of play; toggling between addition and subtraction, each time a player uses a name beginning with a letter R (or any preferred initial letter).

NUMBER BOND COUNTDOWN

RECALL AND CONSOLIDATION OF NUMBER BONDS

This game is played in a circle. It requires children to give pairs of number bonds in sequence by listening to the previous player's response and taking one off the first number and adding it to the second. If play began with number bonds of 10, the children's responses would begin thus:

'10 add zero is 10', '9 add 1 is 10', '8 add 2 is 10', etc.

9

When '**zero add 10 is 10**' is reached play switches to number bonds of 9, beginning with '**9 add zero is 9**' and so on. Continue, dropping down a set of bonds each time a 'zero add . . .' is reached. Children who give a wrong response or hesitate are out and fold their arms to indicate they are out of the game to those still in play. Those remaining in play must pay ever-closer attention to make sure they don't hesitate.

Variations
- Start at a higher set of number bonds (e.g. number bonds of 20).
- Start with low sets of number bonds (e.g. number bonds of 5) and increase the bond set each time that 'zero add . . . ' is reached.

ODDS AND EVENS

IDENTIFYING ODD AND EVEN NUMBERS

For this game you need a large box of Unifix® or similar cubes that click together.

First, each child picks up cubes in each hand and fixes them together into a stick. They then have to break their stick of cubes in two, those who can make two even sticks join the 'evens' group, those with two non-matching sticks (i.e. they have an odd number of cubes) join the 'odds' group.

Next the children have to find a partner from their own side (odd or even). If they can't find a partner from their side they are out. This presents the opportunity to draw attention to a group having an odd number of children.

Each pair of partners joins their cubes together in one long stick. One of each pair breaks the stick into two behind his/her back and their partner chooses one part. They break away from their partner and join either the 'evens' or 'odds' group according to how many cubes they now have. Again, children who cannot find a partner in their group are out. The pairing up and separating process is repeated until either time runs out or a small number of children remain in play.

STAND UP AND BE COUNTED (1)

PLACE VALUE WITH INTEGERS

This activity requires a computer and interactive whiteboard. Divide the class into two, three, four or even five groups, each assigned to a place value column (i.e. 'hundreds', 'tens', 'units', etc.).

Create an Excel spreadsheet file (as outlined below), and use the 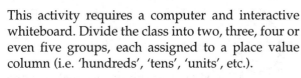 key to generate sets of digits. Each time you press the key, you call out one of the numerals displayed. The group assigned to that place value column must all stand up, call out its value (e.g. 'fifty') and sit down straight away.

After a few goes change the place value columns that are assigned to each group.

 Use the same random number generator as the one described in **Order Them**, but use cells that are adjacent.

Variations
- Give each group member an order of play number so that only one person is meant to stand and call.

- Eliminate any wrong callers or late callers from the activity.
- Give each group two place value columns to monitor.

STAND UP AND BE COUNTED (2)

PLACE VALUE WITH INTEGERS AND DECIMALS

This game is played in the same way as **Stand Up and Be Counted (1)** and with the same variations. You will need to stress the importance of articulating the values carefully with all those 'ths' on the ends of the decimal values.

Again you will need to use an Excel file to create the random numbers, and you will probably want to use five or more digits.

How to set up the decimal version:

- Make a copy of the spreadsheet used for **Stand Up and Be Counted (1)** and paste it onto another sheet in the same file, **Chapter 6** will tell you how to do this if you're not too sure.
- Add in extra cells with the **=RANDBETWEEN(A1,B1)** formula.
- Insert a column where you want the decimal point to be, about 20 pixels wide. To create a conventional British decimal point, hold down the (ALT) key and type in **0183**. Give it the same font size as the numerals.

Just as before, each press of the (F9) key changes the digits.

Variations

- Use integer and decimal columns (e.g. 'tens', 'units', 'tenths', 'hundredths', 'thousandths').
- Give groups an integer and a decimal column to monitor.

MAKE A NUMBER

MAKING NUMBERS OUT OF NUMERALS

Sort the players into two or three teams, sitting in parallel rows facing the front. Each round only involves the player at the front of each team. Each team has a section of whiteboard or flipchart on which to write answers.

For each round display two, three or four randomly selected numerals (depending upon age). These numerals can be selected from a set of shuffled cards, (including duplicates), or by making a simple computer-based random number generator as described below.

Upon the word 'go' the front player from each team dashes over to their board and writes down either the highest or lowest number, as directed by you, when you say 'go'.

The first player to correctly write down a number as specified drops out and moves to their team's 'home' area, the others join the back of their team. Play continues until one team gets all their players home.

 You can use the same random number generator as described for **Order Them** – so long as you remembered to save it!

Variations
- Instead of highest or lowest number ask for an odd or even number.
- Ask for both highest and lowest numbers possible from the numerals.
- Ask for the highest odd/even or lowest odd/even number possible.
- With older children go as far as five numerals.

JOIN UP (1)

MAKING SETS, REMAINDERS

This game requires an open area that allows free movement, ideally a school hall. It can also be used as a warm-up for PE or drama. The children walk freely about, perhaps in a style you specify (e.g. *creeping into the house without waking anyone, like a giant with a headache*). As soon as you shout out a number they each have to get into a group of that number and sit down. Children who are without a group are eliminated, and can then help you to choose the next number to call. If a group of the wrong number of children sits down they are also eliminated. The survivors resume their movement.

You can give clues along the lines of: 'There were six groups of four left which makes 24 of you, next time there will be another four out', before calling out 'Fives!'. Play continues until you are down to the last two or three children.

Variations
- Stipulate that each group must have at least one boy and one girl.
- Ban the children from joining up with anyone who was in their last join-up group.

MULTIPLE SNAP

IDENTIFYING MULTIPLES

This game *can* be played using a set of shuffled number cards (as in **Number Lotto**); but it is easier if you can use the simple random number generator in an Excel file running on your computer, and, if possible, connected to your interactive whiteboard.

Split the pupils into two teams and give each team a name. Choose a number whose multiples are being searched for. When they spot a multiple of the chosen number, pupils shoot up their hands to answer, calling out their team name. If they are correct the caller can choose a member of the other team to join theirs. If they are wrong the other team can choose one of the caller's team to join them instead. (They would probably not wish to choose the caller who gave a false response!)

Continue for an agreed time limit or until one of the teams is reduced to an agreed minimum number of players.

 To make your own multiple random number generator, follow these simple instructions:

- Open up MS Excel.
- Type **1** in cell A1 and **60** in cell B1.
- In cell D8 type in **=RANDBETWEEN(A1,B1)**
- Adjust the font size, column widths and row height as described in **Chapter 6**.
- Put a border around cell D8 (again refer to **Chapter 6**).
- Save the file for future use.

Each time you press the 🄵🄹 key a random number will be displayed. You can change the range of the random numbers generated by changing the values in cells A1 (the minimum number) and B1 (the maximum number).

Variations
- Set the random number generator to go beyond 10 times the target number.
- Use the random number generator to find multiples of a multiple of 10 (multiples of 50, 60, 70, etc.) by adding ***10** to the formula in cell D8 thus: **=RANDBETWEEN(A1,B1)*10**.

PRIME TIME

PRIME NUMBERS, FACTORS AND REMAINDERS

This game is cyclical, so if the players are not in a circle a sequence of play must be established (e.g. 'Down this row, across and up this row and back to the start').

The object of the game is for players to give a prime number without repeating one that has already been given. The first player names a prime number and the second gives a pair of factors (not including 1), for the number that is one less than the prime number. The difference between the factors is used to bypass players. For example:

Player 1 names 57 (as a prime number),
Player 2 responds with 4 and 14 (as factors of 56),
The next 10 people are bypassed.
Player 3 continues play by naming another prime number.

Any player giving a non-prime number, or one that has already been used is eliminated from the game. Play continues for a fixed time period, or until a specified number of players is left.

NUMBER VOLLEYBALL

COUNTING ON AND BACK BY A FACTOR OF 10

This game requires two teams, each sitting in a row on opposite sides of the room. Play progresses down the two team rows.

The game begins with the first player calling out a single-digit number to the first player in the opposite team who responds by multiplying it by 10. The number is bounced back and forth between the teams. If no-one slips up the number continues to increase by a factor of 10 until it exceeds 1,000,000,000. From this point the number is reduced by a factor of 10, crossing the zero threshold until it reaches three decimal places. When three decimal places is reached play reverses again, returning to the original single-digit number. The next player restarts play by 'serving' a fresh number.

A strict time limit of a few seconds should be applied. When a player slips up, by either hesitating or giving the wrong response, they drop out and play resumes from the opposite team beginning with a fresh single-digit number.

Play continues until a team has lost an agreed number of players, or until time has run out, in which case the winning team is the one with the fewer lost players.

Variations
- Begin with a two-digit number.
- Alter the upper and lower limits.
- Increase/decrease by a factor of 20.

FIZZ BUZZ

QUICK RECOGNITION OF MULTIPLES AND SQUARE NUMBERS IF USING 2ND VARIATION

This traditional party game, which is played around a circle, exists in a number of variations. The basic principle is that players count around the room substituting a nonsense word for particular multiples.

Count normally around the group *but* use the word 'Fizz' for multiples of 3, 'Buzz' for multiples of 5, and 'Fizz Buzz' for multiples of both.

For example the counting sequence should go:

1, 2, fizz (3), **4, buzz** (5), **fizz** (6), **7, 8, fizz** (9), **buzz** (10), **11, fizz** (12), **13, 14, fizz buzz** (15), **16, 17, fizz** (18), **19, buzz** (20), **fizz** (21), **22, etc.**

Players who slip up, usually by missing the key word or taking too long are eliminated. Play continues until you are left with just one player.

Variations
- Use different multiples (e.g. 4, 6) with alternative nonsense words.
- Add in square numbers, so that 9 becomes '3 squared', 16 becomes '4 squared', 25 becomes '5 squared', etc.

HOSTAGE ROUND UP

ROUNDING NUMBERS UP AND DOWN

The object of this game is to practise rounding numbers. Before play commences you must establish which nearest value numbers are to be rounded to. The players are arranged into two teams. Each round involves only one player from each team. The players in each team are numbered to determine which two are competing for each round. Play begins with the two players numbered '1', then continues with the number 2s, 3s, 4s, etc.

For each round a number is displayed. The two active players compete to be the first to round the number up or down and call it out.

If the first player to call out is correct the other player is taken 'hostage'; but if he/she gives the wrong answer he/she becomes a hostage of the other team. Hostages do not take any further part.

Numbers can be on ready-made cards as numbers, created by drawing out shuffled numeral cards, written up on a whiteboard, or selected using random number generation on a computer.

 To make your random number generator:

- Open up Excel.
- Type a lower limit for your random numbers into cell A1 (e.g. 1), and an upper limit in cell B1 (e.g. 100).
- In cell D10 type the formula:
  =RANDBETWEEN(A1,B1)
- Choose a much larger font size. (Refer to **Chapter 6** for how to do this.)

Each press of the (F9) key will display a fresh random number.

Variations
- Depending upon the age group vary the number to round to the nearest 5, 10, 20, 50, 100, 500, 1000.
- Round measurements to nearest 50 cm, metre, kilometre, 100 g, 500 g, kilogram, tonne, etc.

ROUNDING AROUND

ROUNDING NUMBERS UP AND DOWN

This game is a standard oral game played in rounds, eliminating players who hesitate, stumble, or give a wrong response. You need to use the same random number generating files as for **Hostage Round Up**.

Everyone sits in a horseshoe arrangement, where they can see the random number generator. For the first round the players have to round the displayed number to the nearest 10. Second round to the nearest 20, then round by round, to the nearest: 50, 100, 200, 250, 500 then 1000. Apply a strict time limit to each player; silent counting on the fingers of your hand is effective.

Continue to play until only a few players remain or time runs out.

PERCENT SNAP

RECOGNISING EQUIVALENT VULGAR FRACTIONS AND PERCENTAGES

You *can* play this game using two sets of cards held and turned by helpers; but there are disadvantages such as card preparation, fumbling with cards, dropping them, getting them mixed up, etc. However the main disadvantage is the lack of pace which is possible if you use a computer and your interactive whiteboard to generate the fractions and percentages at the touch of the (F9) key.

To make it easier to identify the first player to 'Snap!' you can specify that they must stand up as they 'Snap', and/or call out their name/team name instead of the word 'Snap'.

You can operate this activity in three different ways:

- In teams (no more than three or four). Points are awarded for each correct Snap but deducted for false alarms.
- In two teams where a correct Snap captures a member of the other team, as outlined in **Multiple Snap**.
- As individuals, as outlined in **Number Snap**.

 How to make a Snap game for tenths and percentages in multiples of 10 per cent:

- Open up MS Excel.
- Type 1 in cell A1 and 10 in cell B1.
- Type **=RANDBETWEEN(A1,B1)** in cells C1 and B8.
- In cell G8 type **=C1*10** and put a % sign in H8.
- Give B8 a thick bottom border (see **Chapter 6**) and type 10 in cell B9.

- Adjust column and row sizes as follows (instructions on how to do this are also in **Chapter 6**):
  - ○ column B **150** pixels wide,
  - ○ column G **200** pixels wide,
  - ○ column H **100** pixels wide.
- Highlight rows 8 and 9 and change the font size to **72**.
- Hide the contents of cells A1, B1 and C1 by changing their font colour to white.
- Use the ▤▤▤ icons to **centre** column D, and align column G to the **right** and H to the **left**.

Each press of the Ⓕ⁹ key will change the fraction and percentage.

How to make a Snap game for hundredths (in multiples of 5) and percentages in multiples of 5 per cent.

- Copy/paste the Percent Snap game onto a new sheet in the same Excel file (refer to **Chapter 6** if you're not sure how).
- Make the following changes
  - ○ Add ***5** to the formula in cells B8 and C1 like this: **=RANDBETWEEN(A1,B1)*5**
  - ○ Widen column B to 200 pixels.
  - ○ Change cell B9 to **100**.
  - ○ Change cell G8 to **=C1**.

Variations
See the choices given in the game instructions above.

Use multiples of 2 rather than of 5 by changing the ***5** in cells B8 and G8 to ***2**. Note: this will mean a much lower rate of matches.

DECIMAL SNAP

RECOGNISING HUNDREDTHS IN MULTIPLES OF 5 WITH THEIR DECIMAL EQUIVALENT

This is played in the same ways as **Percent Snap** but seeks to match with equivalent decimal values rather than percentages. Again you *could* manage using masses of prepared cards instead of a computer and interactive whiteboard; but why subject yourself to all that hassle when a simple Excel file will do all the hard work for you?

To make your hundredths/**Decimal Snap** game:

- Open up the Percent Snap files in MS Excel.
- Change B1 to **19**.
- Change B8 and G8 to **=RANDBETWEEN(A1,B1)*5**
- Change B9 to 100.
- Insert a conventional decimal point in F8 by holding down the (ALT) key while you type in **0183**, and delete the % sign from H8.
- Adjust column and row sizes as follows (instructions on how to do this are also in **Chapter 6**):
  - columns B and G **200** pixels wide,
  - column E **100** pixels wide,
  - column F **30** pixels wide.
- Use the ▦▦▦ icons to **centre** column D, and align column E to the **right** and G to the **left**.
- Each press of the (F9) key will change the fraction and decimal.

To add a sheet which compares percentages with decimals:

- Copy/paste the hundredths/decimals Snap game onto a new sheet in the same Excel file (refer to **Chapter 6** if you're not sure how).
- Make the following changes
  ○ **Delete cell B9.**
  ○ Remove the bottom line border from B8.
  ○ Type the % symbol in cell C8 and change the width of column C to 100 pixels.
  ○ Align cell B8 to the right and C8 to the left.

CHAPTER 2
Calculations

TEAM PROMOTION

QUICK MENTAL COMPUTATION OF ADDITION AND SUBTRACTION EQUATIONS

Arrange two teams of children in parallel rows facing each other as shown below. Lay out number flashcards in front of each team member 1 to however many team members there are.

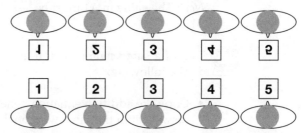

Show the children an equation, which has an answer that comes within the range. The two children with that answer on their flashcard hold it up as quickly as they can. The first to do so is 'promoted' up to number 1 position in their team, requiring some team members to move down one place to fill the space he/she has vacated. Continue play for a fixed time or until most/all the children have had a turn in the number 1 position.

Equations can be on a set of flashcards, written up on a whiteboard, or generated using the simple Excel file shown below.

 To make your own computer **addition** equation generator:

- follow the simple instructions for the Snap game in **Number Snap**, but insert a space followed by the + sign in cell E8, and a space followed by the = sign in G8. *Note*: you must insert a space *before* you type in the + and = symbols.
- Make these two symbols larger and centre them.

To make the equations harder increase the values in cells A1 and B1.

Note: The value in A1 must be less than the value in B1.

 To add a **subtraction** equation generator to the file, do the following:

- Copy the addition equation generator onto a new sheet in the same workbook file – instructions are in **Chapter 6**.
- Type in 1 in cell A1 and 11 in B1.
- In cells C1 and F8 type in **=RANDBETWEEN(A1,B1)**
- Change the font colour of C1 to white in order to hide it.
- Change D8 to **=C1+F8**
- Replace the + in cell E8 with a space followed by the − sign.

Each time you press the Ⓕ⁹ key a new equation will be generated. You can change the range of numbers by altering the numbers in cells A1 and B1.

Variations
- Use a strict time limit for responses.
- Penalise wrong answers by sending the culprit down to the bottom of his/her team, promoting some team members up one space to fill in the space vacated.

SWAP OVER

QUICK MENTAL COMPUTATION OF ADDITION AND SUBTRACTION EQUATIONS

This game is a variation of **Team Promotion**. The children are playing as individuals, not as teams. However, they need to sit in two rows facing each other. The positions in each row are numbered from opposite ends, so that the two with the number 1 are diagonally opposite. The children have to remember the position they currently hold.

When an equation is given, the two children sitting in that position (one from each row) must get up and attempt to swap places. The child who sits down last goes to the end of the row (the highest numbered position) and the rest of the row move up one place to fill the empty space. *Example*: You give the equation 10 – 4 and children sitting in position 6 in each row try to swap places. The child who is last to sit goes down to the end of the same row, e.g. position 14, and children previously in positions 7 to 14 all move up one place. Play continues for a fixed time, as there is no overall winner.

Variations
- Treat the two rows as teams – instead of swapping places use a chair placed in the centre between the rows which both children have to try and sit on, rather like the last round in

Musical Chairs. The successful player scores a team point.

- Both players go to the end of the opposite row rather than the other player's position, allowing some to move up.

FIRST TEAM HOME

QUICK MENTAL COMPUTATION OF ADDITION AND SUBTRACTION EQUATIONS

Children sit on the carpet grouped into two or three teams. Each team has a 'home' area, ideally a set of chairs close by.

Display a number on a flashcard. The children put up their hands when they have thought of a number sentence which has that number as its answer. The first child to give a correct answer goes to their team's 'home'. The first team to have all their players in their home area is the winner.

Variations

- A wrong answer brings back into play the member of that team who has been in the home area the longest.
- In addition to giving the children the answer, give them another number to include, e.g. 'Use 5 and another number to make 8.'

LEAGUE TABLE (1)

QUICK MENTAL CREATION AND COMPUTATION OF NUMBER EQUATIONS

The players sit in a horseshoe arrangement and each player's position is numbered from 1 upwards. Each player needs to remember their number, as labels are not permitted.

Play begins with the highest-numbered player calling out a number equation, the answer to which must be less than his or her own number.

For example, if the first player calls out 35 ÷ 5, the player in position 7 must respond by raising a hand or standing up. They are then allowed a few seconds to reply with an equation of their own, passing play on to whoever is sitting in the position of the answer.

A player is deemed to have transgressed if they: (a) fail to respond quickly enough to their number being the answer, (b) respond when their number isn't the answer, (c) give a follow-up equation with an answer that is their own number, or (d) give a follow-up equation with an answer greater than the highest number in play.

Transgressors are relegated to the last number, causing the players below them in the league to move up a place.

Play continues for a fixed time period, players aspire to finish up in the top 4 or 5 places.

Variations
• Restrict play to one of the four rules.

- Specify which rules can be used by which players, such as:
  - odd numbers must add, even numbers must subtract;
  - positions 1 to 10 must multiply, 11 to the end must divide.

LEAGUE TABLE (2)

QUICK MENTAL CREATION AND COMPUTATION OF NUMBER EQUATIONS INCLUDING NEGATIVE NUMBERS

The rules and method of play are the same as for **League Table (1)** but with the following adaptations:

The player at the centre of the horseshoe is numbered 'zero', players to their left are numbered positively from zero, and those to their right are given negative values.

Players on the positive side of zero who transgress (as outlined in **League Table (1)**), take the place of their negative counterpart, who in turn joins the end of the positive section. Players below the transgressor's vacated place all move up one. Players on the negative side of zero who transgress are simply relegated to the end of their section. The object is to end up as zero or close to it on the positive side.

JOIN UP (2)

ADDITION OF SETS

This game needs a reasonably large open space.

The children are allowed to sit themselves down in groups of 1, 2, 3 or 4. Play starts when you call out a number greater than 4. Groups have to find another group to unite with to form a group corresponding to the number you called out. For example, if you called out 'Six!' a group of 3 would seek out another group of 3 while a group of 4 would be looking for a group of 2. Any groups not united into a group of the required number are eliminated.

Each united group must then split up into two new smaller groups before play recommences.

Variations
- Specify that start-up groups have to be odd or even numbers.
- Specify that there must be at least one boy and one girl in each united group.

TARGET TOTALS (1)

ADDITION

This game requires a set of cards numbered from 1 to the number of players.

It also requires a space that will allow for free movement.

Shuffle up the cards and distribute them.

When you call out a target total the players have to join up with others in 2s, 3s or 4s so that the total of their number cards equals the target total and sit down together. Each time some players will be left standing without a match. Check off that each seated group has achieved the target total.

Target totals should be in the range of (number of players + 1) to (number of players × 2).

Make the next target total closer to the other end of the suggested range.

Variations
- Collect up, shuffle and redistribute the number cards.
- Only use even numbers as target numbers so that each group requires two players with an odd-numbered card.
- Specify a maximum number of players in each target total group.
- Do not allow players to group with anyone they grouped with last time.

TARGET TOTALS (2)

ADDITION

This is played in the same way as **Target Totals (1)**, **but using** two cards of each number. For example 30 players would require two sets of cards numbered 1 to 15.

Target totals should be in the range of (number of players + 1) to (number of players × 2). The number of players without a target total group will vary each time.

Variations
- Insist that each group includes a *double* (i.e. two players with the same number).
- Specify a maximum number of players in each target total group.
- Do not allow players to group with anyone they grouped with last time.

HALVES AND DOUBLES

HALVING AND DOUBLING

This game is played around in a circle. The object is to gradually eliminate players until only an agreed number remain in play. This game toggles between sequences of halving and doubling numbers. Play begins with a high even number (e.g. 100). Numbers are halved until an odd number is arrived at. This triggers a changeover, the next player subtracts 1 from the odd number, thereafter play is switched to doubling the number each time.

When a player cannot double without exceeding an agreed limit (e.g. 1,000), they subtract 4 and play then switches back to halving.

A typical sequence might go as follows:

100, 50, 25, $^{(25-1)}$ 24, 48, 96, $^{(96-4)}$ 92, 46, 23, $^{(23-1)}$ 22, 44, 88, $^{(88-4)}$ 84, 42, 21, $^{(21-1)}$ 20, 40, 80, $^{(80-4)}$ 76, 38, 19, etc.

Wrong responses, pauses, or being caught 'napping' eliminate players from the game, and they indicate they are out by adopting an agreed posture (e.g. arms folded, sitting on floor instead of chair, etc.)

When a player is out the previous player re-starts by repeating their last response.

Variations
- Re-start following each elimination from a different number nominated by you.
- Alter the upper limit for doubling, for example allow doubles up to but not exceeding 200.

NUMBER CRICKET (1)

DOUBLING NUMBERS, TOTALS TO 5 DIGITS

This game requires two teams, each sitting in a row on opposite sides of the room. One team bowls and the other bats before swapping over. You need to act as umpire, keeping the score and a tally of how many players are 'out'.

The first bowler 'bowls' to the first batsman by calling out a 2-, 3- or 4-digit number. The batsman must call out its double within a strictly applied time limit of 3 to 5 seconds. If the batsman fails to do so correctly they are out. If they respond correctly within the time limit they score runs according to the number that was bowled.

2-digit number scores 1 run
3-digit number < 500 scores 2 runs
3-digit number > 500 scores 3 runs
4-digit number < 5,000 scores 4 runs
4-digit number > 5,000 scores 6 runs.

Each batsman plays once in an innings, requiring each opposing bowler to bowl once. In the second innings players who were out do not bat.

The winning team is the one that scores the most runs. In the event of a tie the team with the fewer lost wickets wins.

Variations
- Allow 5-digit numbers that are multiples of 50, worth 6 runs.
- Allow a slightly longer response time when more difficult numbers are bowled.
- Teams select a limited number of batsmen from their squad for the first innings. Second innings must be drawn from the remainder of the squad.

NUMBER CRICKET (2)

HALVING NUMBERS, UP TO 4 DIGITS

This game is played in the same way as **Number Cricket (1)**. The difference is that the batsman has to halve the number that has been bowled at them.

The response time(s) allowed may have to be adjusted. Runs scored are as follows:

2-digit even number scores 1 run
2-digit odd number scores 2 runs
3-digit even number scores 2 runs

3-digit odd number scores 3 runs

4-digit even number scores 4 runs

4-digit odd number scores 6 runs.

Variations

- Allow 3-digit, 1 decimal place numbers worth 6 runs.
- Allow a slightly longer response time when more difficult numbers are bowled.
- Teams select a limited number of batsmen from their squad for the first innings. Second innings must be drawn from the remainder of the squad.

NUMBER ROUNDERS

SEQUENTIAL DOUBLING

This game is played in two teams, in a similar way to **Number Cricket**.

The first team to bowl may only bowl odd numbers ranging from 1 to 29. These numbers are written up on a whiteboard and marked off by you acting as umpire when they have been bowled. You also need to keep a tally of rounders scored.

The purpose of only bowling numbers once is so that the bowling team can save the more difficult numbers to bowl at more able pupils; thus differentiating according to the relative abilities of the batting team.

When a number is bowled the receiving batter has 15 seconds to score a rounder by doubling it four times. For example if the number 3 is bowled the batter must reply with 6, 12, 24, 48 in order to score a rounder.

When play switches to the other team the bowlers may only bowl even numbers ranging from 2 to 30.

The object of the game is to score rounders.

Variations
- Increase the response time allowed, perhaps according to the size of the number bowled.
- Specify a different set of numbers that can be bowled.
- Have a second innings involving the players who scored a rounder, but with a shorter response time.
- Play with decimal numbers.

DOUBLE UP

DOUBLING UP, TOTALS UP TO 4 DIGITS

This game requires an order of play to be established (e.g. 'Down this row, across to Nigel and up the middle row, across to Tracey, down to the back and start again at the beginning').

The first player gives a number that is less than 20. Subsequent players double the number given by the previous player, until the number exceeds 1,000. When 1,000 has been exceeded the next player nominates another start number; but this must not be one already used. Strict observance of a time limit for each player is necessary. The easiest way of doing this is to count seconds silently but openly on your fingers.

Wrong answers, hesitations and proposing a start number already used will eliminate a player from the game. Play on until only an agreed few are left.

Variations
- Use higher or lower starting numbers.
- Use a higher threshold for re-starting.
- Use only multiples of 10 or 100.

EIGHTS AND NINES

USING SHORTCUTS TO QUICKLY ADD AND SUBTRACT 9 AND 8 MENTALLY

The pupils sit roughly in a circle, or else you establish a circular order around the room and back to the start, each player adding to (or subtracting from) the previous number.

A pupil starts by calling out a number within a range prescribed by you.

Each pupil's gender determines which number they must add. Begin with female pupils adding 9 and males adding 8. Toggle this each time play passes the start so that all players practise adding both numbers. If you have a single-sex group, use a different criterion, such as hair length/colour.

Wrong answers and unacceptably slow responses put the pupil out of the game.

Variations
- Use the (–10, +1) and (–10, +2) shortcuts to subtract 9 or 8.
- Include negative numbers, crossing the zero threshold.
- Switch between addition and subtraction on a given signal, either from you, or when a player adds or subtracts the wrong number.
- Reverse the direction of play on your signal.

EIGHTIES AND NINETIES

USING SHORTCUTS TO QUICKLY ADD AND SUBTRACT 90 AND 80 MENTALLY

This is played in the same way as **Eights and Nines**, but using the (+100, –10) and (+100, –20) shortcuts.

Variations

* Use the (–100, +10) and (–100, +20) shortcuts to subtract 90 or 80.

* Include negative numbers, crossing the zero threshold.
* Toggle between addition and subtraction on a given signal.

NUMBER BOND TENNIS

NUMBER BONDS OF 100, 200, 500, 1,000

Divide the class into two teams, preferably sitting on opposite sides/ends of the room. This game is based roughly around the rules of tennis. Team members are numbered and take turns at serving and receiving serve in their number order.

Play begins with one team's player number 1 'serving' – calling out a number less than 100 – to the receiving team's player number 1.

The 'receiving' player must respond by calling out the number that would make it up to 100, within a strict 5-second time limit. (This time limit is best done by holding up a hand as you silently count on your fingers.)

If the receiver responds correctly within time they win the point and now serve to the next player in the other team. If the receiving player gives the wrong answer or runs out of time the server wins the point, and serves again, this time to the next player.

This game uses tennis's curious scoring system: 15, 30, 40, ('advantage'), 'game'. Due to time constraints it is better to play up to a time limit rather than first team accrue six games won in a set.

Variations
• Use number bonds of 200, 500 or 1,000.
• Adjust the time limit for responses.
• Allow a team captain to nominate who is to serve or receive serve next, while not using any player twice until all have been used once.

FIBONACCI COUNT

ADDING ON IN SEQUENCES

This game is based on the work of the Italian mathematician Leonardo Fibonacci (1170–1250). In 1202, while hypothesising about generations of rabbit reproduction, he came up with the sequence of numbers that bears his name. It is based on the number of pairs of rabbits doing what rabbits do naturally (their grasp of maths is limited to multiplication!), while taking mortality into account.

The sequence consists of adding on the last two numbers like so:

$$1, \overset{0+1=}{} 1, \overset{1+1=}{} 2, \overset{1+2=}{} 3, \overset{2+3=}{} 5, \overset{3+5=}{} 8, \overset{5+8=}{}$$
$$13, \overset{8+13=}{} 21, \overset{13+21=}{} 34, \overset{21+34=}{} 55, \text{ etc.}$$

Players will have to sit around in a circle. The object is to eliminate players down to an agreed number, as described in **Halves and Doubles**.

You will need to start off the sequence and nod to the first player for them to continue.

Begin by saying: 'Zero and one makes one, one and one makes two, one and two makes three'.

Each time a player falters, the sequence starts again: 'Zero and one makes one'.

Variations
- Since Fibonacci is no longer around to sue you for misrepresenting his work, start off from a different number; but still adding the previous two numbers to get the next.
- Use triangular numbers (visualise the red balls on a snooker table) whereby you simply add one more than you added last time:

$$0, \,^{0\,+\,1\,=}\,1, \,^{1\,+\,2\,=}\,3, \,^{3\,+\,3\,=}\,6, \,^{6\,+\,4\,=}\,10, \,^{10\,+\,5\,=}\,15,$$
etc.

- Make a goal of seeing how high the class can get before faltering.

CHAPTER 3
Measurement

TIME JUMP (1)

ADDING ON INTERVALS OF TIME

This game is cyclical, so if the players are not in a circle a sequence of play must be established.

Play begins with the first player giving a time in hours and minutes, using such as 09:30. Each subsequent player adds on a specified time interval, for example 20 minutes. Players must respond by adding on the time quickly, or else they are out. Each time play reaches the start the time interval is changed, to something slightly more difficult. For example you might begin adding 20 minutes, then 15, 45, 40, 35, 25, 18, etc.

Variations
- The start time makes a big difference, for example commencing at a multiple of five minutes is much easier say than starting at 09:58.
  - Play the game backwards in time.
  - Use both 12- and 24-hour clock times.
  - Go past midnight.

TIME JUMP (2)

ADDING ON INTERVALS OF TIME

This is best played using only the 24-hour clock. Begin as for **Time Jump (1)**; but instead of keeping a time interval for each complete circuit it is increased for each player as follows:

Player 1 gives a start time, player 2 adds 5 minutes, player 3 adds 10 minutes, player 4 adds 15 minutes and so on.

Variations
- Play the game backwards, taking off increasingly large time intervals.
- Play forwards or back beginning with high interval (several hours), and reducing by 5 minutes each go until the interval reaches zero, then start to increase again.
- Use a computer and interactive whiteboard to quickly emulate the additions of varied time intervals, as described below.

 To calculate the increasing time intervals and correct answers

- Open up a new Excel file.
- Highlight the entire sheet by clicking on the corner between the column and row labels.
- From the **Format** menu select **Cells, Number, Custom.**
- Type **hh:mm** into the custom box
- Type **Interval** into cell A1, **00:05** into cell A2 and **00:10** into A3.
- Highlight cells A1 and A2 together as shown here, and with the mouse drag down on the tiny black square in the bottom right-hand

corner of the pair of cells, as far as row 30 or even further. This has quickly given you time intervals increasing in 5-minute increments.

- Type a start time (e.g. **09:35**) into cell C1, and in C2 type **=C1+A2**
- Select cell C2, place the cursor over the bottom-right black square and holding the left mouse button drag down to the same row as you did for column A.
- If you change the start time in cell C1 the rest of column C will update.

TIME VOLLEYBALL (1)

ADDING INCREMENTS OF TIME

This game requires two teams sitting in rows facing each other. Play progresses from player to player down the two team rows.

To begin play you specify a time increment and a start time. The first player in the team that starts adds on that time increment, and then the first player in the other team responds by instantly adding the increment, passing play to the second player in the first team. When a player slips up by not responding instantly with the correct time they are out, and play restarts with the next player of the other team, with a new start time. When play reaches the end of the team that started the round, you begin a new round beginning with the other team, using a fresh start time and changed time increment.

Play continues until one of the teams has been whittled down to an agreed number.

Variations
- Instead of eliminating players who slip up, award a point to the opposing team, and play on for a number of rounds or period of time.
- Vary the time increment to match the level of the players; perhaps in multiples of 15 minutes for younger players, progressing through to increments that are near multiples of 10 minutes.
- Work backwards, deducting the time increment.

TIME VOLLEYBALL (2)

ADDING ON INCREASING INCREMENTS OF TIME

This game is a variation of **Time Volleyball (1)** and is played in much the same way. The major difference is that the amount of time added on by each player increases by 5 minutes each time. The first player adds 5 minutes, the second 10 minutes and so on until a player slips up.

When a player has slipped up and been eliminated, you nominate a fresh starting time for the next player on the other team, who then re-starts play by adding 5 minutes.

Variations
- Play the game for points rather than eliminating players.
- Play backwards, deducting increasing periods of time.
- Toggle between adding and subtracting time on each occasion that a player slips up.
- Use start times that will lead to crossing over midnight.
- Specify strict use of 24-hour clock times.

- Specify use of 'minutes to' and 'minutes past' rather than just hours and minutes.

CROSSING THE RIVER

PROBLEM-SOLVING WITH MASS

This is a group activity; pupils have to work in pairs to come up with a solution.

The winning group is the one that comes up with a viable plan using the fewest trips. As a tie-break you can take order of finishing into consideration.

The initial scenario is that a family needs to get across a river with a small boat that will only safely carry 90 kg. The family comprises:

Dad (80 kg), Mum (60 kg), Baz (50 kg), Trace (40 kg) Tim (30 kg) and Fang their Labrador puppy (20 kg) who must be restrained by a non-rower when in the boat.

Variations
- To make the task more straightforward, explain that family members can cross back across the river – they do not have to stay on the opposite side.
- Increase the capacity of the boat to 100 kg, 120 kg.
- Add 40 kg of camping equipment that cannot row itself!
- Let the kids bring a friend or two along!

BRAINSTORMING MASS

CHOOSING APPROPRIATE UNITS OF MASS

Divide the players into teams of three or four. Give each group a slip of paper and tell them to appoint a scribe and to write their chosen team name on it. Explain the need to discuss quietly so that others do not hear.

First round: ask them to write down five things that would be best weighed in kilograms. Collect the slips and discuss any clearly impractical suggestions – challenge everyone if appropriate to convert an approximation into the suggested units. For example, if they suggested using grams to weigh a bus (usually around 9–10 tonnes), let them divide by 1,000 to convert to kilograms, then by 1,000 again to convert to tonnes. Use this as an opportunity to draw attention to a tonne being a million grams.

Each sensible item that the other groups have not also written down scores a point.

Repeat with further rounds using tonnes, grams and, possibly for older groups, milligrams.

Total up point scores to decide which team won.

Variations
- Apply a strict time limit for each brainstorm, perhaps as short as a minute.
- Vary the number of items requested.
- Add another condition, such as: an animal 'could be found in a house', 'could fit in a carrier bag'.
- Ask for suggestions as to what instrument to use to measure the weight.

BRAINSTORMING LENGTH

CHOOSING APPROPRIATE UNITS OF LENGTH

This is basically the same game as Brainstorming Mass but using units of length such as metre, centimetre and millimetre. To avoid ribald comments it is advisable to restrict suggestions to inanimate object, e.g. something made of metal.

Variations
- Use imperial units of length.
- Discuss accurate ways of measuring, such as callipers, micrometer.
- Discuss varying need of accuracy, for example compare road direction mileage signs with building plans.

BRAINSTORMING VOLUME

COMPARING VOLUMES AND CAPACITY

This is also a variation on **Brainstorming Mass** but using units of volume such as millilitre (ml), cubic centimetre (cc), centilitre (cl) and litre.

Brainstorm 'what might you buy . . . in plastic litre bottles, glass bottles, 5-litre plastic containers, from a pipeline, etc.'

Brainstorm which units would be best to measure medicine, recipe ingredients, liquid fuel (e.g. petrol), water for a fish tank, etc.

Note: in very large quantities, water is often measured in tonnes – 1,000 litres of pure water weighs 1 tonne.

RAPID CONVERSION (1)

CONVERTING MEASURES IN LARGER UNITS TO THE EQUIVALENT VALUE IN SMALLER UNITS OF MEASURE

This game requires the Excel file described below, ideally displayed on an interactive whiteboard. The object is to develop the rapid conversion of larger units to smaller by using place value changes to multiply by 100 or 1,000.

Divide the class up into two teams. Players each take a turn at representing their team, so they need to be numbered to establish their order of play. Assign a 'recording table' with scrap paper and a felt-tip pen to each team.

For each round a randomly generated value is displayed using a large unit of measure such as in kilograms, litres or metres. This is done by pressing the (F9) key.

To begin play the (F9) key is pressed and the two active players must go to their team's recording table, write down the equivalent value in the appropriate smaller units (e.g. grams, millilitres or millimetres), and hold up the paper. The first player with the correct conversion is deemed to be 'home' and drops out of active play. Answers can be checked using the Excel file by pressing the **Page Down** key, returning to the top of the sheet for the next go by pressing **Page Up**.

Play can be stopped after everyone has had one go, declaring the team with the most 'home' as the winner. Alternatively, you can have a second round involving only those who did not make it home first time.

Follow these instructions to make a file that converts kilograms into grams by multiplying by 1,000:

- Type the following into the cells identified:

in A1	100
in B1	999
in D30	=RANDBETWEEN(A1,B1)
in D2	=D30/1000
in A30	=D2
in E2 and B30	kg
in E30	g

- Widen columns A and D to 300 pixels and columns B and E to 150 pixels.
- Change the font size of D2, A30 and B30 to 72 and the size of E2, B30 and E30 to 48.
- Format cells D2 and A30 to Number with 3 decimal places.

To practise converting tonnes to kilograms, metres to millimetres, kilometres to metres, litres to millimetres, simply change the unit abbreviations in cells E2, B30 and E 30.

To add a sheet to your file that converts metres to centimetres by multiplying by 100 change cell D2 to =D30/100.

For this file to work you need to have the **Analysis Toolpak** *Add-In* enabled. For help doing this look in **Chapter 6**, under 'Excel-specific hints'.

Variations
- Add extra sheets to your files, each containing different versions of the above, so that you can change from one to another simply by clicking on the sheet tabs at the bottom of the screen. **Chapter 6** tells you how to do this.
- Allow the two competing players to go to their recording table before you hit the (F9) key.

- Allow the teams to confer and to send a different team member to their recording table each time. With this variation teams score points and you can end either when a team reaches a predetermined score, or else when the allotted time runs out.

RAPID CONVERSION (2)

CONVERTING MEASURES IN SMALLER UNITS OF MEASURE TO THE EQUIVALENT VALUE IN LARGER UNITS

This game is played in the same way as **Rapid Conversion (1)** and with the same variations. If you have already made and saved the **Rapid Conversion (1)** Excel file you can quickly adapt a copy by following the instructions below.

Amend your **Rapid Conversion (1)** file for use with **Rapid Conversion (2)** to match the spreadsheet below.

How to make a file that converts grams into kilograms:

- Type the following into the cells identified:

in A1	**100**
in B1	**999**
in D2	**=RANDBETWEEN(A1,B1)**
in D30	**=D2/1000**
in A30	**=D2**
in E2 and B30	**g**
in E30	**kg**

- Widen columns A and D to 300 pixels and columns B and E to 150 pixels.
- Change the font size of D2, A30 and B30 to **72** and the size of E2, B30 and E30 to **48**.

51

- Set the format of cell D30 to **Number** with **3 decimal places.**
- Make sure that cells D2 and A30 are set to **0 decimal places.**

Variations

- Use the variations described for **Rapid Conversion (1).**
- Add extra sheets to your file and change the unit abbreviations to convert
  ○ kilograms to tonnes
  ○ millimetres to metres
  ○ millilitres to litres.
- On extra sheets, change cell D30 to **=D2/100** and alter the unit abbreviations to convert
  ○ centimetres to metres
  ○ centilitres to litres.

CHAPTER 4
Shape and Space

SHAPE LOTTO

RECOGNITION OF REGULAR SHAPES

Use a set of 20 or so pairs of cards with shapes. Use shapes such as: circle, ellipse, equilateral triangle, isosceles, scalene, square, long oblong, fat oblong, parallelogram, pentagon, hexagon, octagon, trapezium and rhombus. Place them face down on the carpet in rows.

As with **Number Lotto**, each child has a go at turning over two matching cards. If they match, the child keeps them and becomes a spectator. If they don't match, the cards are turned face down again. Play continues until all the cards are paired up. Ask the children how many goes they needed before they found a pair, and who didn't find any. Discuss the properties that distinguish similar shapes from each other, such as right angles, pairs of parallel lines, etc.

This game can also be used to promote spatial awareness and classification skills.

Variations
* Increase the number of cards available by using more shapes or by including duplicate pairs.
* Vary the size and orientation of the shapes on the cards.

- Have two games going on at once, racing to see which group of players finishes first (without cheating!).

SHAPE SNAP

RECOGNITION OF REGULAR SHAPES

For this game you can use the same set of cards as for **Shape Lotto**, perhaps with more duplicates in the set.

Arrange the children into two teams identified as 1 and 2, with a space between. You sit at one end between the teams, and two non-playing helpers stand apart at the other end, one in line with one of the teams.

The cards are shuffled and dealt face down into two piles.

Each helper holds up a pile with the bottom of the pile showing.

To dictate the speed of play you instruct the helpers when to change cards by simply calling '1, 2, 1, 2' and so on. Cards are changed by removing the facing card and placing it on their own discard pile.

When a child sees a matching pair they shout their team number and shoot up their hand. You adjudicate as to who was first and that team wins the other team's discard pile to add to the back of their card pile. Play continues until one team loses by running out of cards.

Variations
- Use extra cards.

54

- Vary the size and orientation of the shapes on the cards.
- Allow different types of triangle to be paired together.

TRIANGLE LOTTO

CLASSIFICATION OF DIFFERENT TYPES OF TRIANGLE

Use a set of cards face down on centrally placed tables. The card set should include 15 of each of the following types of triangle: scalene, equilateral, isosceles, and non-isosceles right-angled. Vary the size, proportions (where applicable), and orientation.

Use some of the turnings-over to highlight the properties that distinguish or match up the cards. Paired cards do not have to be identical; they merely have to be the same type of triangle.

Variations
- Play as individuals (as with **Shape Lotto**).
- Play as teams, team members taking turns, to see which team collects most pairs.

TREASURE HUNT (1)

LETTER AND NUMBER COORDINATES

For this game you need 36 identical-looking cards, 35 of them blank and one with a drawing of a treasure chest on its reverse. You also need smaller column labels A to F and row labels 1 to 6 – for ease these can be written on two long strips of paper.

Lay out the column and row labels.

Shuffle the cards and lay them down to fit the column and row labels.

A player nominates a card by its coordinates, and you or a non-playing helper turns the card in that position over. If it is the treasure card, that player or team has won – if it's too quick, reshuffle, re-deal and play again!

Variations
• Play as teams, members taking turns.
• Use more cards by adding rows and/or columns.
• Leave the turned cards face up or turn them over again.
• Have more than one treasure card.
• Play as teams and use an odd number of treasure cards – the team that finds more wins.

TREASURE HUNT (2)

2-DIGIT NUMBER COORDINATES

This game is played like **Treasure Hunt (1)**, and can be played with the same variations. The difference is that you use conventional 2-digit number coordinates.

To facilitate this you need a pre-drawn large grid with the grid lines labelled either 0, 1, 2, etc., or 00, 01, 02 and so on. The cards need to be small enough to fit on the intersections of gridlines without obscuring the grid itself.

Make sure that the first coordinate is always from the x-axis. The children can make up ways of remembering to use the horizontal axis first, such as 'Go in the house . . .' (finger walk along the *x*-axis) '. . . and up the stairs' (finger 'climb' up the grid).

Record on a whiteboard each pair of coordinates tried, using the conventional (2, 3) style of notation. In addition to keeping a note of what has been tried, it gives the opportunity to point out where players have mistakenly nominated the *y*-axis first.

TREASURE HUNT (3)

2-DIGIT NUMBER COORDINATES, ALL FOUR QUADRANTS

This is played in precisely the same way as the preceding versions of **Treasure Hunt**. It differs in that you use all four quadrants with both the *x* and *y*-axes labelled – 6 through to + 6, and intersecting at 0.

Players have to nominate points on the grid by specifying whether each value is positive or negative.

Again use conventional notation (e.g. (– 3, + 4) to record which positions have been tried.

PIPELINE (1)

DIRECTIONS

Play requires a grid of large squares, displayed on whiteboard, flipchart or overhead projector slide. The object is for a number of teams to construct a pipeline across the grid, either West–East or East–West.

Identify four to six teams and give them a starting position.

For each turn a dice is thrown and the score indicates the sort of move they can make as follows:

1 = 1 square NE, NW, SE or SW
2 = 2 squares NE, NW, SE or SW
3 = 1 square E or W
4 = 2 squares E or W
5 = 1 square N or S
6 = 2 squares N or S

The team calls their choice of move to a marker who draws in on the grid. The first move is from their nominated starting point on the edge of the grid. Subsequent moves are added on to the previous move.

The pipelines are not to touch or cross, so if the choice of move available cannot avoid doing so the team must miss its turn.

The first team to cross wins.

DON'T LOSE YOUR BEARINGS

BEARINGS

For this activity everyone needs a copy of the same grid as for **Pipeline (1)** on cm^2 paper. If you wish you can include x and y-axes for easier identification of positions. Display a reminder of the compass points that bearings in multiples of 45º correspond to.

0°	45°	90°	135°	180°	225°	270°	315°
N	NE	E	SE	S	SW	W	NW

The object of this activity is for the whole group to devise a route around the grid, arriving back at or near the starting point. Beginning from an agreed starting point, each pupil in turn names a bearing and everyone marks that move on their own grid. Each move is of one square, be it vertical, horizontal or diagonal. For checking purposes the bearings should be written down in sequence. When everyone has added their bearing to the route they can be compared. How many people have finished up in the 'correct' location? How close is it to the starting point?

Variations
- Allow/don't allow the route to cross itself.
- Insist on a fast pace.
- Allow/don't allow the use of compass directions instead of bearings.
- Allow pupils to work as pairs.

PIPELINE (2)

COORDINATES

Prepare a 12 × 12 grid and number the x and y-axes 0 to 12.

The object of the game is for two teams, each working in two halves, to build a pipeline across the grid without crossing the other team's pipeline.

The teams are North and South, and East and West, their names denoting the general direction of their pipeline.

Play follows the order: North, East, South, West.

When it is their turn each half-team names two adjoining grid positions between which a section of pipe is drawn, for example (3, 7) to (4, 8).

The teams are not allowed to add to the section they put in place on their previous move.

If a team crosses a section of the other team's pipeline they must miss a turn to allow for the extra time needed to bridge over the obstacle. The first team to complete wins. If both teams complete on the same round then the team that crossed the other's pipeline loses.

PIPELINE (3)

COORDINATES IN ALL FOUR QUADRANTS

The game proceeds in the same way as for **Pipeline (2)**; but with the following variations:

- The playing grid is placed around the intersecting x and y-axes.
- The North group starts from the + end of the y-axis.
- South group starts from the − end of the y-axis.
- East group starts from the + end of the x-axis.
- West group starts from the − end of the x-axis.
- Pipelines can cross over at the zero point on the intersecting axes.
- Pipelines are allowed to cross an axis.
- Pipelines cannot be laid on top of an axis.

CHICKEN PEN

PERIMETER AND AREA

This is a collaborative brainstorm activity done as teams of three or four.

You need to have prepared for each team an identical set of three or four slips of paper, with lengths written on them, such as 16 m, 24 m, 36 m and 56 m.

The task is for the team to quietly decide the dimensions for the largest-area chicken pen they could make using that length of wire netting. When they have written their team name and chicken pen dimensions down, a team member returns the slip to you and collects the next one, and so on.

The order of completion of the last slip is noted.

For each of the slips, each team's dimensions are checked to make sure that the perimeter equals the length of netting available. If correct the area of the proposed pens are compared, earning the team(s) with the largest area a point. Team points are totalled. If two or more teams have the same highest number of points, use the order of completion of the last slip to decide the overall winner.

Variations
• Give dimensions in centimetres.
• Allow half-metres to be used.

SHAPE UP

PERIMETER AND AREA OF POLYGONS

This is a team-based quiz involving rapid but quiet collaboration.

For each of four or five rounds you give the team the perimeter of a *regular* polygon in centimetres. They have to brainstorm out what shapes it *could* be and the lengths of the sides. Half-centimetres are permissible.

It is advisable to prepare the perimeters and the possibilities for each before you go into the classroom, as this will make scoring much easier.

For example, if you gave them a perimeter of 36 cm they could have:

an equilateral triangle (6 × 12 cm), square (4 × 9 cm), hexagon (6 × 6 cm) or an octagon (8 × 4¹/₂ cm).

Allow one or two minutes per round. Teams can swap papers for checking, 1 point available for each correct polygon with correct side length.

Variations
- Use larger perimeters.
- Use different units of length (millimetres, metres).
- Give perimeters as decimals of a metre.

CHAPTER 5
Data Handling

NAME A ... (1)

VENN DIAGRAMS

Draw a pair of intersecting Venn rings, labelling one 'Girls' and the other 'Dark hair'. Identify the properties of each area of the diagram (as below).

Girls   Dark hair

girls with light hair   girls with dark hair   boys with dark hair

boys with light hair

Assign a different coloured cube to represent each area of the diagram. You also need a bag or box containing cubes of the same colours.

Each child takes a cube without looking, and then has to name someone who fits the criteria for the part of the Venn diagram assigned that colour of cube. If the suggestion is correct it is written down on the diagram.

Variations
• Children score a point by making a correct suggestion.
• Children play singly or in teams.

- Children unable to make a correct suggestion
  (e.g. if all the boys with dark hair have been
  suggested already) are 'out'.
- Change the criteria for the rings (people who
  can swim/ride a bike/are wearing .../stay for
  dinner/can tie laces, etc.

NAME A . . . (2)

CARROLL DIAGRAMS

This game uses a Carroll diagram with two criteria,
such as the one shown below.

	hot	cold
drink		
food		

The game is conducted in the same way as **Name a
... (1)**, with coloured cubes used to determine which
criteria the child's suggestion has to meet.

A time limit for a correct suggestion is applied.
Children are eliminated from the game if they
cannot give an appropriate suggestion in the time
allowed.

Variations
- Change the criteria.
- Play the game in teams – the last team with
  players remaining wins.
- Play the game in teams – the team with most
  correct suggestions wins.
- Use a criterion with 3 options, such as: goes
  home for dinner, brings a packed lunch, has a
  school dinner.

SHAPE SORT

CARROLL DIAGRAMS

This is a team task to see which team can correctly place a set of cards in the correct sectors of a Carroll diagram. Each team will require a Carroll diagram grid, with columns labelled with the names of colours, and rows labelled with the names of shapes. Removable labels will make changing the criteria easier.

Have prepared a set of cards depicting each of the shapes in each of the colours. Vary the sizes and orientation of the shapes.

Shuffle the cards and deal 8 to each team. The first team to complete correctly wins the round; but an error will lose them the round.

Retrieve the cards, re-shuffle and re-deal for subsequent rounds.

DATA RELAY

QUICK PROCESSING OF MEAN, MEDIAN, MODE AND RANGE

Players are split up into teams of 4.

For each team the game organiser has a set of three 'data' slips similar to the illustration below.

The first member of each team is given their first slip face-down. The remainder of their cards are left on an identifiable face-down pile at the front of the room.

On the word 'go' the first player in each team works out and writes in the range and passes the slip face-down to the second player, who completes the mode before passing it on to the third player (median). Scrap paper is allowed for working out.

When the fourth member of the team has written in the mean they keep it face-down, signalling that the first player can fetch their next data slip from the team's pile.

When all three slips have been completed a team member returns them to the organiser, who records the order in which the teams returned the completed slips. Each team's slips are compared with the correct answers and the first team to have completed all slips (or most slips) correctly is the winner.

Sample sets of data:

3	1	8	2	3	4	7
8	12	8	17	15	22	9
3	21	21	14	19	20	21
24	31	24	41	11	18	19

Variations
- Omit the mean from the data slip.
- Vary the number of data – an even number is more challenging when working out the median.

- Differentiate the size of the data to give everyone a range of difficulty, or to suit the ability of individual teams.
- Change the team play order each time so that each performs a different task on each slip.
- Allow the teams to confer.

PROBABILITY BRAINSTORM

PROBABILITY

For this activity you need a set of cards with events written on them and a probability scale such as one of the ones illustrated below, depending upon age range.

◄—— less likely			more likely ——►	
no chance	poor chance	even chance	good chance	certain
0		½		1

impossible	evens	certain
0	.5	1

Present the cards one at a time, reach a consensus about where they should be placed on the scale and stick them on with the inevitable bit of blue sticky stuff.

When discussing the probability of an event, compare it with the probability of other events already on the scale; you may want to re-position some in relation to others.

Suggestions for 'events':

The sun rising, eating Christmas pudding today, completing the lesson's tasks, winning the lottery, eating chips today, being kidnapped by aliens, washing a teacher's car, buying crisps today, having a bath this week, going home today, being knocked over by a bus, eating meat today, rain/snow/hail/thunder today, foreign holiday today, the teachers' lottery syndicate winning the jackpot and all retiring, Manchester United winning the FA Cup, Blackburn Rovers winning the FA Cup, Accrington Stanley winning the Premier League this year.

Plus anything else suitably topical.

Variations
With younger children it is probably reasonably safe to let them suggest possible/impossible events. As the age of the group increases, the probability of insensitive, insulting, lewd and downright disgusting suggestions rises rapidly to the 'certain' end of the scale.

CHAPTER 6
ICT Tips and Hints

COMMON TO MOST/ALL MICROSOFT APPLICATIONS

Font sizes
Normally you select your font size by clicking on the drop-down arrow which forms part of the font size icon 12 ▼ and selecting the size you want. However, you can select sizes that are not displayed there. To do this highlight the size which is in the font window, type in a number and press (Enter).

Using characters that are not on your keyboard
Most fonts have many more characters than your keyboard has buttons for. Many can be typed by holding down the (ALT) key while you type in a 4-digit number. Below are some examples with their code number.

$\frac{1}{4}$ (0188) $\frac{1}{2}$ (0189) $\frac{3}{4}$ (0190)   · (0183)   ÷ (0247)   ° (0176)

To find other examples open up Windows Character Map 🌢. In some versions of Windows you can drag a character from the Character Map window straight into Word or Excel.

Using Wingdings and other 'picture' fonts
These special fonts have characters that are pictures, and they can be very useful. The examples on the next page are all taken from the original Wingdings font, and are illustrated with the keyboard letter that they correspond to.

☺ J　　☹ K　　☹ L　　🎤 M　　🗿 N
☎" 　📖 &　　☎ (　　🖥 :　　🗔 r

Keyboard shortcuts

Cut, copy and paste

Instead of using the mouse to cut, copy or paste you can use keyboard shortcuts. Hold down the (CTRL) key and press **X**, **C** or **V**. You will notice (as illustrated below) that the letters appear on the keyboard just as they do on the taskbar.

This is a very useful technique (a) because it avoids taking your hand away from the keyboard to wiggle your mouse, and (b) because you can use it in applications where you don't have these functions on a taskbar. It's useful for pasting from one application to another.

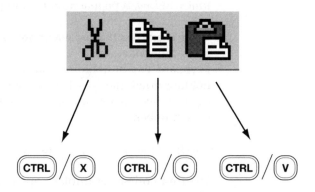

Other keyboard shortcuts

You can use (CTRL) / B, I, and U to toggle **Bold**, *Italic* and U̲n̲d̲e̲r̲l̲i̲n̲e̲d̲ text on and off instead of using the **B** *I* U̲ icons. You can use (CTRL) / Z to undo.

Format Painter

To quickly change a font to the style, size and colour you've already used elsewhere in Word or Excel:

Highlight part of the text you want to use as an example, copy it to the clipboard, then click on the **Format Painter** icon 🖌 and brush across the text that you wish to change.

EXCEL-SPECIFIC HINTS

Generating random numbers
The formulae used in the game instructions to generate random numbers on each press of the F9 will not work if Excel on your computer does not have the **Analysis ToolPak Add-In** enabled. To correct this click on the Tools menu, select **Add-Ins** then tick the box for **Analysis ToolPak**.

Selecting more than one cell, row or column at a time
This is a useful trick if you want to apply the same style, font, font size, font colour, background colour or format to all of them at the same time.

- Click on the first cell, column label or row label.
- Hold down the CTRL key and click on the others.

If the columns or rows you want to select are adjoining, you can do so by simply dragging the cursor along the column or row labels.

If you wish to multi-select adjacent cells just drag the cursor across them.

Using very large fonts
When you have a much larger, easy-to-see-at-a-distance font size it is necessary to adjust the column width and row height. Choose a much larger font size and adjust the column width and row depth fit. You *could* go up to a font size of **250**, requiring a column width of around **850** pixels to fit a 4-digit number, and a row depth of around **300** pixels.

Column width and row depth

To alter the column width, drag your mouse on the join between two column labels: ▭ D | E ▭ . As you do so the width in pixels will be displayed next to your cursor. This is useful if you need to match the width with other columns.

To change the width of two or more columns together, highlight them either by dragging along the column labels, or by multi-selecting by holding the (CTRL) key as you click on each column in turn. Drag out on one of the selected column labels as described above.

To alter the depth of a row, select it by clicking on the row label then drag on the join between it and

the next row label: 8 / 9 . As you do so the depth of the row in pixels will be displayed.

To change the depth of more than one row at a time select them in the same way as you did for changing column widths.

Hiding the grid

The spreadsheets described in this book will look better if you hide the grid. To do this click on the grid icon ▦ which is on the **Forms** toolbar. If this toolbar is not displayed click on View , select **Toolbars** and click next to **Forms**.

Working with workbook files and sheets

Excel files are referred to as *workbooks*, and they can contain one or many spreadsheets. On most computers Excel is set up to include several sheets, accessed by clicking on the tabs at the bottom of the screen. \ **Sheet1** ⟨ Sheet2 ⟨ Sheet3 ⟩ .

This means that each of the spreadsheets suggested in this book could be saved in the same file.

Naming sheets

To make such a workbook more user-friendly you can rename the tabs by double-clicking on them so that they might for instance be called

\Number Snap / Order Them / Stand Up & be counted / Stand Up DECIMAL version / .

Copying an entire sheet onto a new spreadsheet

It's often useful to copy and paste an existing spreadsheet onto a new sheet and then adapt it.

- Select an entire sheet by clicking on the grey rectangle in the corner between the column and row labels: .
- Use (CTRL) / (C) to copy the spreadsheet, click on a tab to select a new sheet, make sure cell A1 is selected, then use (CTRL) / (V) to paste.

Excel cell formats

The default format for cells is *General*, but often it is useful to change the format by clicking on Format and selecting **Cells** . . .

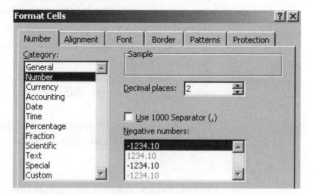

This brings up the range of categories of format which you can click on to get more options. The illustration on page 73 shows the options for **Number**, enabling you, among other things, to set the number of decimal places. Some categories enable you to specify symbols, separators and order (e.g. US month/day or European day/month).

The **Currency** category allows you to select/not select decimals and currency symbols.

The **Custom** category allows you to specify what you want, and this is very useful if you wish to have an hours and minutes format. This is good if you want Excel to add, subtract, multiply or divide measures of time, for example working out time intervals.

Select **Custom** and type in **hh:mm** in the Type box like this:
.

This example will set the format to hours and minutes, each displayed as two digits.

Date format
On some computers Excel has not been set to use European date formats, and defaults to the American month/day/year. This can cause confusion when the day number is 12 or less, for example in American format, 05.06.02 means 6th May but in UK format it means 5th June. To correct this follow the **Custom** instructions above; but inserting either of the following variations:

d.m.yyyy to give day, month and 4-digit year.
dd.mm.yyyy to always give 2 digits for the day and month.

If you prefer, use a / as a separator instead of a full stop.

Borders
To put a border around a cell first select it then click on the drop-down arrow which forms part of the border icon ▦ ▾ and select the border you want. For example you can add a thick bottom border, as suggested for cell B8 in **Percentage Snap** by selecting the ▥ icon.

Alternatively you can click on the **Format menu** and select **Cells** then **Border**. This gives you a greater range of options, including colours and broken lines.

Foreground (text) colours
Select the cell(s), click on the drop-down arrow on the font colour icon **A** ▾ and choose a colour.

Using colour to hide text
If you don't want students to see the value you have typed in a cell, such as the maximum range for random number generation, simply use the same font and background colour.

Background colours
To colour individual cells select them, then click on the drop-down arrow that forms part of the background colour icon ▨ ▾ and select a colour.

Using the Fill function
Time
The **Fill** function creates sequences of values or words. It can save the drudgery of working out intervals of time and dates. For example, when the dreaded parents' night is approaching, why not try this on your classroom PC:

- Open up Excel and in a cell enter the time of the first appointment. In the cell below put in the time of the second one.

- Now highlight the two cells, put the cursor over the drag handle in the bottom right hand corner of the lower cell ![03:40 / 03:50] and drag downwards with the left mouse button. Excel's **Fill** function will fill in further appointment times using the same time interval.
- If you are one of those people who like to work backwards, enter the times of your last two appointments then drag upwards to create the preceding appointment times.
- Now just make the rows a bit taller, and widen the column for names.

Now you can hand over appointment booking to the kids; so long as you regularly save and back up the file.

Dates
You can automatically **Fill** lists of dates in a similar way. When you input the date, use a forward slash / to separate day, month and year. Enter two dates (e.g. consecutive or a week apart), highlight them and left-click drag on the handle.

Note: Assuming the second date is the later one, dragging downwards produces later dates. Dragging upwards will produce earlier dates instead. Filling a series of times or dates works across rows as well as down columns; useful if you want dates or times as column headings.

You may want the dates to be filled for just weekdays, or for months or years. To achieve this highlight just *one* date and drag on this drag handle with the *right* mouse button. A mini menu box will appear and give you the choice of filling by Days, Weekdays, Months or Years – just choose what you want.

Numbers
The **Fill** function is also useful to create sequences of numbers such as multiples. If you enter 1 in a cell, 2 in the next, highlight then drag, you'll get 1, 2, 3, 4, 5, 6, etc. If the two highlighted cells contain 1 and 3 the result will be odd numbers – 1, 3, 5, 7, 9, etc.

To make a list (however long) of multiples of 7 use 7 in the first cell and 14 in the second.

You can fill several columns at once if you wish. For example, dragging down on this selection  will produce a 9 times table. *Note:* When inserting the = sign as a character you must insert a space before it; otherwise Excel will think you are starting inserting a formula.

Computing with periods of time
In the format periods of hours and minutes can be added, subtracted, multiplied and divided.

When a time total exceeds 23 hours and 59 minutes it will move on to 1 day 0 hours and 0 minutes. You can prevent this from happening by inserting square brackets around the hours like this **[hh]:mm**.

Here is an example of how you could use Excel to calculate journey times. Complete cells **A1:E1** as shown below, put the formula **=d1-b1** into **F1**, and format cells **B1**, **D1** and **F1** as described above. Changes to the departure and arrival times will result in the journey time being recalculated automatically.

	A	B	C	D	E	F
1	leave at:	09:30	arrive at	14:17	Journey time:	4:47

You can do the same trick vertically. If you want to be awkward and have a journey that runs overnight (i.e. into the next day), you'll need to add 24 hours to the time, so for an arrival at 01:35 the next day enter **25:35**.